WHEN
the SKY
GLOWS

Nell Cross Beckerman
ILLUSTRATED BY **David Litchfield**

Beach Lane Books

NEW YORK LONDON TORONTO SYDNEY NEW DELHI

Around the world,

when morning comes ...

the sky glows.

Emerging at dawn, a **sunrise** looks especially colorful to our night-adjusted eyes. When the sun is low on the horizon, the sunrays travel through longer distances, so colors with short wavelengths like blues and greens are filtered out, leaving warm yellows, oranges, and reds.

On a lake by the equator,
when clouds crack . . .

the sky glows.

Lightning forms from thunderclouds filled with static electricity. Lake Maracaibo in Venezuela is called "the lightning capital of the world," where bolts sometimes strike over a thousand times per hour in a nearly continuous electrical storm.

On a tropical misty island,
when raindrops stop . . .

the sky glows.

Rainbows appear when sunrays bend as they pass through raindrops, causing the colors to separate. Hawaii is known as "the Rainbow State" because the combination of wet weather and sunny skies produces so many rainbows.

In the zone of totality,
      when the moon blocks the sun...

the sky glows.

Although a total **solar eclipse** happens somewhere on Earth every eighteen months, total eclipses visit the same area of the world only once every few hundred years. The "zone" or "path" of totality is the darkest area on land during the eclipse.

At a watering hole on a delta,
when shadows grow ...

the sky glows.

Photographers love the golden light at **sunset**. Harsh
midday sun can cause very bright and very dark spots,
making a good photograph hard to light. The reddish indirect
glow of sunset lights photographs more evenly, while the low
angle of the sun also causes longer, more dramatic shadows.

In the land of fire and ice,
when high peaks pop . . .

the sky glows.

Volcano eruptions happen when molten rock, called "magma," rises from deep within Earth's core through the volcano to the surface. The heat makes the magma glow, and we call it "lava." Iceland has about 130 volcanoes, and although many are extinct or dormant, some have active explosive eruptions.

Along a steamy wooded path,
when dusk descends . . .

the sky glows.

There are over 125 types of **fireflies** in the United States. For two weeks every June, a rare breed of firefly flashes in sync during mating season in the Great Smoky Mountains National Park, making a natural light show in the trees.

Around a beach bonfire,
when stars shimmer . . .

the sky glows.

A **meteor shower** is made of debris from a passing comet
traveling through Earth's atmosphere. The speed of the leftover
pieces of comet causes friction with the air, leaving glowing
streaks also known as "shooting stars" or "meteoroids."

Far from city lights,
        when the air feels fresh and frosty...

the sky glows.

Auroras light up the night sky with greens, pinks, and blues, occurring when electrically charged particles from the sun enter the Earth's atmosphere. Aurora borealis and Aurora australis—"the northern lights" and "the southern lights"—are seen close to the North and South poles in areas like Scandinavia, Canada, and New Zealand.

All around the world,
when busy days end...

the sky glows.

A **full moon** can seem as bright as a light bulb, but unlike
a light bulb, the moon is reflecting light, not producing it.
The sun's rays bounce off the moon and cause it to shine.
A full moon appears roughly once every month, depending
on the position of Earth between the moon and the sun.

Until morning,
   when the sun rises once again . . .

and the sky glows.

Thank you to the CBs, Deborah Halverson,
Kim Turrisi, and SCBWI. Dedicated with love
to my family, and all skywatchers.
—N. C. B.

For my art teacher Mr. White, who taught me
how to find inspiration in the world around us.
—D. L.

CAN YOU SEE THE SKY GLOW?

Lots of us see sunrises and sunsets, but can't see many stars and the full wonders of the night sky because of **light pollution**. Cities and towns are too bright at night. Light pollution makes it hard to see stars, comets, and auroras, and can damage and disorient wildlife and disrupt our own sleep cycles.

We can help reduce light pollution by asking our cities and towns to use special light-directing streetlamps, and by reducing our own outdoor lighting. A portion of the author's proceeds from this book will be donated to the **International Dark-Sky Association**, which works to protect our night skies and find solutions to light pollution. For more information about how *you* can help, visit darksky.org.

SOURCES AND FURTHER READING:

Sunrise and Sunset
Wolchover, Natalie. "Do Sunrises Look Different from Sunsets?" Live Science. July 10, 2012. https://www.livescience.com/34065-sunrise-sunset.html.

Lightning
Falcón, Nelson. "Phenomenology and Microphysics of Lightning Flash of the Catatumbo River." Paper presented at the XIV International Conference on Atmospheric Electricity, Rio de Janeiro, Brazil, August 2011.

Rainbows
Stewart, Melissa. *Why Do We See Rainbows?* New York: Benchmark Books, 2008

Solar Eclipse
Loomis, Ilima, and Amanda Cowan. *Eclipse Chaser: Science in the Moon's Shadow.* Boston: Houghton Mifflin Harcourt, 2019.

Volcanoes
"The Complete Guide to Iceland's Volcanoes." Guide to Iceland. https://guidetoiceland.is/nature-info/the-deadliest-volcanoes-in-iceland.

Fireflies
Leaf, Christina. *Fireflies.* Minnetonka, MN: Bellwether Media, 2018.

Meteors
Schneider, Howard. *Ultimate Explorer Field Guide: Night Sky: Find Adventure! Go Outside! Have Fun! Be a Backyard Stargazer!* Washington, DC: National Geographic Kids, 2016.

Auroras
"What Is an Aurora?" NASA Space Place. Last modified August 12, 2021. https://spaceplace.nasa.gov/aurora/en/.

Moon
Gibbons, Gail. *The Moon Book.* New York: Holiday House, 1997.

BEACH LANE BOOKS
An imprint of Simon & Schuster Children's Publishing Division
1230 Avenue of the Americas, New York, New York 10020
Text © 2022 by Nell Cross Beckerman
Illustration © 2022 by David Litchfield
Book design by Greg Stadnyk © 2022 by Simon & Schuster, Inc.
All rights reserved, including the right of reproduction
in whole or in part in any form.
BEACH LANE BOOKS and colophon are trademarks of Simon & Schuster, Inc.
For information about special discounts for bulk purchases,
please contact Simon & Schuster Special Sales
at 1-866-506-1949 or business@simonandschuster.com.
The Simon & Schuster Speakers Bureau can bring authors to your live event.
For more information or to book an event,
contact the Simon & Schuster Speakers Bureau at 1-866-248-3049
or visit our website at www.simonspeakers.com.
The text for this book was set in Bluberry and Impressum.
The illustrations for this book were rendered digitally.
Manufactured in China
0522 SCP
First Edition
2 4 6 8 10 9 7 5 3 1
Library of Congress Cataloging-in-Publication Data
Names: Beckerman, Nell Cross, 1973– author. | Litchfield, David, illustrator.
Title: When the sky glows / Nell Cross Beckerman ; illustrated by David Litchfield.
Description: First edition. | New York : Beach Lane Books, [2022] |
Includes bibliographical references. | Audience: Ages 0–8 | Audience: Grades 2–3
| Summary: "Sunrises and lightning storms, rainbows and volcanoes, meteors
and fireflies-these beautiful, and sometimes frightening, events that light up
the sky might seem like magic. But there is a scientific explanation for each
natural phenomenon. Find out the science behind the magic in this beautiful and
enlightening nonfiction picture book"— Provided by publisher.
Identifiers: LCCN 2021022431 (print) | LCCN 2021022432 (ebook) | ISBN 9781534450394
(hardcover) | ISBN 9781534450400 (ebook)
Subjects: LCSH: Meteorological optics—Juvenile literature. |
Sky—Juvenile literature.
Classification: LCC QC975.3 .B43 2022 (print) | LCC QC975.3 (ebook) |
DDC 551.56/5—dc23
LC record available at https://lccn.loc.gov/2021022431
LC ebook record available at https://lccn.loc.gov/2021022432